Snow White and the seven dwarfs

Look at the pictures and read the story.

Once upon a time there was a beautiful girl called Snow White. She lived with a queen who was very wicked. The wicked queen had a magic mirror. When she looked in it she said,

"Mirror, mirror on the wall,
Who is the fairest of us all?"

The mirror always replied,
"Thou, queen, art the fairest in the land."

But one day when she spoke to the magic mirror, it replied,

"Snow White, O queen, is the fairest in the land."

The queen was very angry and she told her servants to take Snow White into the woods and kill her. But the servants liked Snow White because she had always been kind and friendly and so they did not kill her but took her to the woods and ran away.

Snow White wandered about the woods, quite lost, until she was so frightened and tired that she lay down under a tree and sobbed herself to sleep.

Seven dwarfs lived in the woods and luckily for Snow White they found her fast asleep under the tree. They carried her gently back to their house and when she woke up they told her she could stay with them.

The seven dwarfs were workmen. They told Snow White their names. Each one had the name of the tool he used to do his work.

The tools

There was Hammer dwarf.

There was Scissors dwarf.

There was Bradawl dwarf.

There was Drill dwarf.

There was Vice dwarf.

There was Screwdriver dwarf.

There was Saw dwarf.

The seven dwarfs decided that as Snow White was going to live with them they ought to build a bigger house, so they asked her to help them.

Snow White wanted to work with them in a team, all solving problems together. So she said, "Yes!"

Before Snow White could begin working on the house she needed to find out about the tools. The dwarfs said they would show her how to use them.

Find out where your tools are kept.

Ask ◆ how you take the tools out
   ◆ how to put them away
   ◆ where you can use them
   ◆ when you can use them

Make sure that your teacher is always around when you use the tools.

Be careful ⚠

Activity 3

Hammer dwarf

Hammer dwarf showed Snow White

his 2 different hammers

his 2 different kinds of nails

his different blocks of wood

Pretend to be Snow White. Find the right nail to go with the right hammer.

Let Hammer dwarf show you how to hammer in a nail safely into a block of wood.

Practise hammering in some nails.

Try different kinds of wood.

Be careful

✱ Why do we use nails?   Collect different nails.

Saw dwarf

Saw dwarf showed Snow White

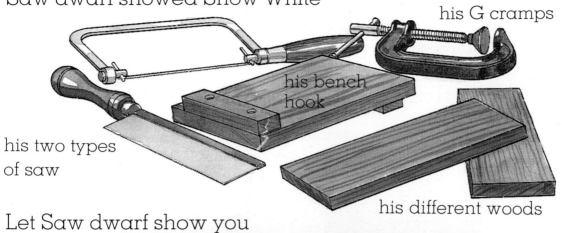

his G cramps

his bench hook

his two types of saw

his different woods

Let Saw dwarf show you

◆ how to make sure the wood is held firmly
◆ how to make sure the sharp edge is pointed away from your body
◆ how to keep your fingers away from the front of the saw

Practise doing some sawing.

Try both saws.

Try different sorts of wood.

Activity 5

Vice dwarf

Vice dwarf showed Snow White his vice.

He told her she could use this for holding all sorts of things.

Let Vice dwarf show you

◆ how to hold the wood firmly in the vice

◆ how to hold a coke can so that you can make a hole with a hammer and a nail

Practise sawing some wood using the vice.

Make sure you

◆ hold the saw downwards slightly.

◆ keep close to the vice when sawing the wood.

Drill dwarf

Drill dwarf showed Snow White how his drill worked.
He told her only to drill when the wood is in the vice.

He showed her

◆ how to put the drill bits in

◆ which way to turn the drill
to make a hole

◆ how to stand the drill in a
drill stand

Practise drilling holes.

Look at the drill
carefully to see how it
works.

Activity 7

Screw dwarf

Screw dwarf showed Snow White his

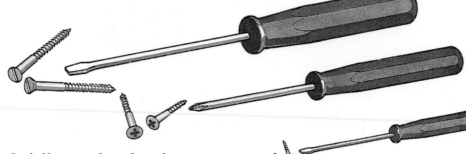

3 screwdrivers

3 different kinds of screws

Pretend to be Snow White and find the right screwdriver to fit the right screw.

Make a model screw.

You will need

plasticine   a nail

✳ How are screws different from nails?

    Look and see.

    Test and see.

Look for nails and screws in your school and at home.

Bradawl dwarf

Bradawl dwarf showed
Snow White his bradawl or
awl.

Let Bradawl dwarf show you

◆ how to use the bradawl
safely so that it is not
pointed at you or near
your fingers

◆ how to make a starter
hole

◆ how to make the hole
bigger using a pencil

Practise using a bradawl to make some holes in other
things.

You will need
objects from the junk box

Sort the objects into easy to do and hard to do.

Activity 9

Scissors dwarf

Scissors dwarf let Snow White try out his scissors.

Some were round-ended.   Some were sharp.

Experiment to find out what they will or won't cut.

You will need

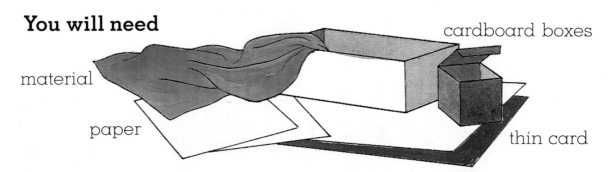

material

paper

cardboard boxes

thin card

✱ Which things were the easiest to cut?

Discuss what makes the scissors cut.

Building the house

Think about what the dwarfs' house might look like. Talk over your ideas.

Prepare to make a model of the house.
Are you working with someone else as a team, like the dwarfs?
Remember that the model must fit in a certain space. Use a space on your table or desk.
Think about the problem.

You will need

objects from
the junk box

tools

Choose an object to be your house. Ask yourself these questions:

✳ Is the size right?   ✳ Can we cut it ?
✳ Does it fit onto the space?   ✳ Can we stick things onto it?

Draw pictures of the house you are going to build.

Activity 11

Working in a team

Snow White and the dwarfs work together in a team. They all have different jobs and help each other.

Can you work together with your friend or friends, all helping each other?

Have you got different jobs?

Talk about your house.

* Have you any problems in making your model?
* Which tools are you going to use to make it?
* Does the house fit into the space?
* Is it going to have a roof?
* Have you changed your ideas from the first drawing?

Draw the house again. Use all the ideas you have come up with as a team.

Paint and colour 1

You will need

classroom paints

paint brushes

Paint a picture of your house with the paints in your classroom.

Talk about colour.

   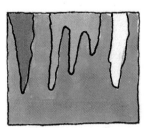

Shades and tones.   Light and dark.

Talk about

happy colours   hot colours   sad colours   cold colours

✳ What other feelings do you have about colours?

Try mixing different colours.

Blue and yellow   red and yellow   red and blue

Experiment with colour.

Try painting on different textures of paper and boxes.

Try wet and dry paint on wet paper.

Try wet and dry paint on dry paper.

✳ What colours do you like best?

Activity 13

Paint and colour 2

Think about how paint can make your house look more attractive.

Paint other materials you have collected such as plastic bottles and boxes.

Try   thick paint
       thin paint
       soapy paint

* What are you painting with? Try a brush or a sponge.

* What other ways can you think of to paint?

Paint your houses.

Talk about the houses you have made and how the dwarfs and Snow White are going to live there.

Let's use varnish

Your house is now painted.
Do you think it would look more attractive if it was varnished?

Why do we use varnish?
They can make objects look more attractive.
They help to protect objects.

Collect

varnished things   unvarnished things

What do you notice about the appearance of varnished objects?

* Do they   shine?
                reflect?

* Are they brighter?
                more attractive?

Ask how you can take care of varnished things.

Some things might look better not varnished. Can you think of any?

Use varnish to finish the model houses.

You will need
for varnish:
multiglue
egg white

Activity 15

Back to the story

Snow White and the seven dwarfs finished their house. They were very proud of it.

Are you proud of *your* house? Make a class display of the finished houses.

Tell the rest of the class about your house.

✷ Explain what problems you had to solve.
✷ Why did you choose a certain material?
✷ Does the house fit into the right space?

Snow White and the dwarfs lived happily in their house. The wicked queen knew that Snow White was still alive. Do you think the mirror told her?

The queen was so upset that she tried to trick Snow White into eating a poisoned apple.

What did Snow White do?
Finish the story.